Easy but Super Delicious Souffle Recipes

The French Secret to Ecstasy

BY - Charlotte Long

© 2022 Charlotte Long. All rights reserved.

License Page

No part of this book and its content should be transmitted in any format for commercial and personal use without asking for permission from the author in writing.

The purpose of the content is to enlighten you and pass cooking knowledge to you in a straightforward way. Hence, the author is not responsible for any implications and assumptions drawn from the book and its content.

Table of Contents

Introduction 5

1. Basic Souffle 6

2. Banana - Chocolate Souffle 8

3. Tinned Peach Souffle 10

4. Twice Baked Cauliflower Souffles 12

5. Passionfruit Souffle 15

6. Herb and Cheese Souffle 18

7. Twice Baked Polenta Souffles 21

8. Mini Chocolate Souffle Cake 23

9. Double Choco Souffle 26

10. Make Ahead Berry Souffles 29

11. Banana - Lime Souffle 32

12. Passionfruit and Banana Souffle 34

13. Choco Almond Souffle 36

14. Twice Baked Goat Cheese Souffle 39

15. Mocha Souffle 42

16. Gruyere Cheese Souffle 45

17. Raspberry Souffle 48

18. Eggless Kiwi Souffle 51

19. Chicken and Cheddar Souffle 53

20. Grand Marnier Souffle 56

21. Lemon Souffle 59

22. Classic Spinach Souffle 61

23. Vanilla Souffle with Ice-Cream 64

24. Potato Souffle 67

25. Carrot Souffle 69

26. Apple Souffle 72

27. Yam Souffle 74

28. Corn Souffle 76

29. Strawberry Ricotta Souffle 78

30. Blintz Souffle 80

Conclusion: 82

Epilogues 83

About the Author 84

Introduction

You may be a learner or an expert in the kitchen, but cooking experiments are fun for all, don't you agree? In this cooking journey of yours, here is another yummy treat to try for you. France is home to such a classic culture and also has one of the most classic dishes in its cuisine. One such French delicacy is the Souffle, an egg-based dish that can either be sweet or savory, depending on how you like it.

Try out your culinary expertise with the souffle varieties, this cookbook offers. Don't worry if you aren't a baking expert, the recipes are too simple and you are going to love them. So, pick out one or you can even try all, and spread the French aroma all over your household. Serve to your beloved ones and see what a big smile it brings to their faces.

1. Basic Souffle

They say variety is the spice of life, but every variety originates from a classic version that will always be the original. This basic souffle recipe is all you need to begin with before diving into its variations. Fluffy on the inside and crispy on the outside, this dish may seem difficult but it's easier than you think.

Ingredients:

- 3/4 cup milk
- 2 tbsp. all-purpose flour
- 4 egg yolks
- 2 tbsp. butter
- 2 egg whites
- 1/2 tsp. salt
- 1/4 tsp. cream of tartar
- 1/2 tsp. pepper

Serving Size - 4

Cooking Time - 30 minutes

Instructions:

Prepare the oven by preheating it to 375 degrees Fahrenheit.

In a medium saucepan, Take the butter and melt over medium-low heat. Add the pepper, salt, and flour to the pan and pour the milk over everything. Stir well for the ingredients to mix and boil. Cook until the mixture is thickened and smooth.

In a bowl, take the egg yolks and beat well, stir in about 1/4 cup of the flour mix into the bowl. Combine the flour mix with the egg yolks. Set aside.

In a separate bowl, add the cream of tartar and beat the egg whites into the bowl till the mixture becomes stiff. Add some of the egg white mixtures into the flour mix and then add the whole flour mixture to the remaining egg mix.

Take 4 cups and pour the mixture carefully into them. You can even use a casserole dish for the same purpose. Put in the preheated oven and let it bake for about 21-24 minutes. Serve when baked, nice and hot.

2. Banana - Chocolate Souffle

Delicious and healthy, a difficult combo to find, isn't it? Not anymore, this banana-chocolate souffle recipe is the perfect dessert option to have on your cheat day. This fluffy treat is going to be convenient for your gluten-free diet as it involves no flour in the ingredients. So go on, try for yourself, and let your mouth have some chocolate fun.

Ingredients:

- 2 large egg whites
- 2 ripe medium bananas, mashed
- 1 tsp. vanilla extract
- 2 tsp. cornstarch
- 3 tbsp. sugar
- 1/4 cup unsweetened cocoa powder
- Cooking spray

Serving Size - 4

Cooking Time - 30 minutes

Instructions:

Prepare the oven by preheating it to 400 degrees Fahrenheit.

Take the vanilla and banana in a medium-sized bowl and mash properly. Add the cocoa powder and cornstarch, and mix everything well.

Beat the egg whites in a separate bowl and sprinkle sugar over it till soft peaks are formed due to the sugar. Take 1/3 part of the egg mixture and combine it with the banana mix. Stir in the rest of the egg mix as well when incorporated well.

Take 4 ramekins and spray them with cooking spray (butter flavored). Scoop the mixture and transfer it into the ramekins. Put in the preheated oven and bake for about 16 minutes.

Take out of the oven and serve the freshly baked souffle.

3. Tinned Peach Souffle

If the peach season is at its peak at your place, you should try this recipe for sure. An elegant and easy dessert can make you fall in love with sweetness even if you aren't a sweet tooth. So, grab some fresh peaches and let your mouth have some fun with this delicacy, the tinned peach souffle.

Ingredients:

- 1 cup canned peaches (chopped and drained)
- 2/3 tbsp. caster sugar (set aside some extra for dusting)
- 4 egg whites
- 2 tsp. cornflour
- 1 tbsp. butter
- 2 tbsp. Grand Marnier
- 2 cups water

Serving Size - 4

Cooking Time - 30 minutes

Instructions:

Prepare the base from tinned peach at first. Take 1/4 cup water in a pan and add caster sugar to it. Cook the sugar evenly and when the color becomes a blond shade add the peaches to the pan. Lower the heat and cook for about 6 minutes.

Make a cornflour slurry by mixing it with about 2 tbsp. water. Pour it into the pan and cook for another minute by stirring continuously. Set aside from the heat and use a blender to make a peach puree. Stir in Grand Marnier to the puree and let it cool down.

Prepare the oven 20 minutes ahead of baking by preheating it to 200 degrees Celsius. Take four ramekins and gently brush them with butter. Set aside in the fridge till needed.

Take the egg whites in a bowl and then whisk them till they form soft peak forms. Add in the remaining caster sugar and about 5 tbsp. of the peach base. Fold the base in the egg white mixture and then pour into the ramekins.

Let the souffle bake for about 10 minutes till they get tall and plump. When ready, take it out of the oven and serve it alongside your favorite dessert.

4. Twice Baked Cauliflower Souffles

As I've already mentioned that souffle can either be sweet or savory, here is a recipe that qualifies as a starter or main course rather than dessert. You may not be a fan of veggies, but this cauliflower souffle is going to be worth the try. So, are you ready to have some cheese fun with cauliflower?

Ingredients:

- 4 eggs, separated
- 1/2 onion, chopped
- 3/4 cup cauliflower, cut into florets
- 2 fresh thyme sprigs
- 1 tbsp. unsalted butter
- 1 bay leaf
- 1 cup milk
- 3/4 cup thickened cream
- 1 cup plain flour
- 1 cup Gruyere, grated

Serving Size - 4

Cooking Time - 1 hour

Instructions:

Prepare the oven by preheating it to 180 degrees Celsius and get 4 ramekins ready by greasing them. In a saucepan, take onion, cauliflower, thyme, milk, and bay leaf. Bring to boil, lower the heat and cook for about 9-12 minutes with the lid partially on. Once the cauliflower seems tender enough, discard the other contents except for the milk and reserved cauliflower.

Clean the saucepan and melt the butter over low flame. Stir the flour in and cook for about 4-5 minutes. Now, pour in the reserved milk from the previous boil and cook for about another 5 minutes till combined and thickened.

Add half the cheese, 1/2 cup cream, and egg yolks to the pan, and whisk until mixed well. Set the pan aside from the heat.

In a food processor, take the cauliflower florets and blend till a smooth puree is ready. Pour the cheese sauce and blend again for everything to get combined.

Take the egg whites in a separate bowl and whisk them till stiff peaks arise. Mix about 1/4 part of the egg white into the cauliflower mix and then gently fold in the whole egg white mix. Pour the mixture into the ramekins prepared earlier and then put inside the preheated oven for about 15-20 minutes until golden and puffed.

Take out of the pan and keep aside to cool and then turn down on the baking tray. Preheat the oven again to 180 degrees Celsius. Add the remaining cheese and cream over the souffle and put them inside the oven till they get fluffy again. Take out of the oven and serve hot with bay leaves.

5. Passionfruit Souffle

Souffles can be tricky to bake but the softness that melts on your tongue when you take a bite is just inexplicable. This passionfruit souffle is so soft that you won't be able to resist yourself from baking more once you try it.

Ingredients:

- 1/2 cup whole milk
- 4 large egg whites
- 1/4 cup granulated sugar, plus more for ramekins
- 1/4 teaspoon freshly squeezed lemon juice
- 3 tbsp. cornstarch
- 1 tbsp. unsalted butter
- 1/3 cup passion fruit puree
- 1 passionfruit, halved, seeds and pulp removed, for serving
- 1 tsp. confectioner's sugar for dusting

Serving Size - 4

Cooking Time - 30 minutes

Instructions:

Prepare the oven by preheating it to 425 degrees. Brush the insides of the ramekins with butter and dust with the granulated sugar. Place inside the refrigerator on a baking sheet until required.

Take a medium-sized saucepan and pour the milk in it and bring to a simmer over medium heat. In a bowl, take the passionfruit puree and cornstarch, and whisk together to combine well. While whisking, add half of the milk into the passionfruit mix and whisk well till it is incorporated into the mixture. Add the passionfruit mixture to the saucepan and then cook while whisking till everything gets thickened after about 3 minutes. Set aside from the heat and whisk the mixture again. Keep covered so that it stays warm.

In a separate bowl, take the lemon juice and egg whites. Whisk till the mixture appears to be foamy. Add granulated sugar while mixing and continue till the formation of soft peaks takes place. Fold in one-third of the egg whites into the passionfruit mixture to loosen it. And then gently mix the remaining of egg white mixture into the passionfruit mixture.

Pour the mixture into the four ramekins evenly. Put inside the preheated oven for about 15-20 minutes and bake until the souffle rise to be fluffy with a firm surface. Sprinkle the confectioner's sugar over the souffle tops. Spoon a portion from the centers of each souffle and add passionfruit pulp and seeds inside.

Serve and enjoy your French delight!

6. Herb and Cheese Souffle

What can be a better appetizer than a cheese burst delight? This cheesy souffle recipe consisting of an herby twist is all you need to satisfy your savory desires. The taste will leave behind will surely make you crave for more, after all, who doesn't like some extra cheese.

Ingredients:

- 4 large eggs
- 4 tbsp. unsalted butter
- 2 cups milk
- 1/4 cup freshly grated Parmesan cheese
- 1/2 pound fresh goat cheese
- 1/2 cup all-purpose flour
- 2 tbsp. minced chives
- 1 bay leaf
- 2 tsp. minced tarragon
- 1 tbsp. minced dill
- Salt and pepper, 1 tsp. each
- 1 tbsp. minced flat-leaf parsley

Serving Size - 4

Cooking Time - 1 hour 30 minutes

Instructions:

Get the oven ready by preheating it to 375 degrees. Brush the insides of a 2-quart souffle dish evenly with Parmesan.

Let the butter melt over medium heat in a saucepan. Stir the flour in to form a smooth paste. Pour 1 cup of milk into the saucepan and place the bay leaf. Whisk constantly in the remaining milk and bring it to a boil. Cook on a low flame for about 8-10 minutes till the sauce gets thickened. Transfer to a bowl and add the salt, pepper, and goat cheese.

Stir the mixture well and then add the egg yolks and herbs to the bowl. In a separate bowl, whisk the egg whites and then mix them with the cheese sauce.

Pour the mixture into the prepared baking tray and then place in the oven for about 40 minutes. Once the souffle is puffed and brown, take them out of the oven.

Serve hot.

7. Twice Baked Polenta Souffles

With the sharpness of Taleggio combined with the classic polenta taste, this souffle recipe is going to be a blast of flavors for you. Just a little bit of effort and you'll have the perfect treat to please your dear ones.

Ingredients:

- 2 1/2 cups of milk
- 5 tbsp. unsalted butter
- 5 tbsp. plain flour
- 4 eggs, separated, plus 2 extra yolks
- 4 tbsp. instant polenta, plus to dust
- 1 tbsp. grated parmesan
- 1 cup pure cream
- 1 1/4 cup Taleggio, rind removed, chopped

Serving Size - 6

Cooking Size - 1 hour

Instructions:

Prepare about 6 dariole molds by brushing them with butter and dusting them with polenta. Also, get the oven ready by preheating it to 160 degrees.

In a medium-sized saucepan, let the butter melt over moderate heat. Stir in the flour and cook for about 4-5 minutes. Pour the milk and mix with the flour. Set aside from the heat and add the polenta. Whisk well and set aside to cool.

In a bowl, take the egg whites and whisk them till stiff peaks form. Mix the egg yolks into the polenta sauce and stir in the egg whites. Pour the mixture into the molds and place inside the oven for about 20-24 minutes until the souffles are brown.

Take it out of the oven and turn it down into a baking tray. Melt cream and Taleggio in a heatproof bowl until the mixture gets smooth. Top each souffle with the Taleggio sauce and dust with parmesan.

Bake for another 20 minutes till golden and puffed. Take out of the oven and serve hot.

8. Mini Chocolate Souffle Cake

Chocolate is, without any doubt, one of the most beloved flavors when it comes to dessert and the same goes for souffles as well. These chocolate souffle cakes are one of the most popular versions of the French dessert. Taste it once and get a taste of pure bliss.

Ingredients:

- 2 tbsp. fat-free milk
- 1 tbsp. all-purpose flour
- 4 tbsp. granulated sugar, divided
- 1 tsp. powdered sugar
- 1/4 tsp. vanilla extract
- 1 1/2 tbsp. Dutch-processed cocoa
- 1 large egg white
- 1 tbsp. butter

Serving Size - 1

Cooking Time - 1 hour

Instructions:

Get the oven ready by preheating it to 350 degrees. Also, prepare the ramekins by brushing butter on the insides and dusting granulated sugar in each one of them.

In a medium saucepan, stir in flour, 2 tbsp. sugar, milk, and cocoa combine everything and bring to cook over moderate flame for 2 minutes. Stir continuously to make the mixture smooth. Transfer the chocolate mix to a bowl and let it cool down for about 5 minutes. At last, add the vanilla extract and stir the mixture.

In a separate bowl, take the egg whites and whisk properly till stiff peaks form. While mixing, add the remaining sugar into the egg whites and whisk properly. Mix the chocolate mixture with the egg white mix by first folding 1/4th of the egg mixture into the chocolate mix. And then gently mix the complete egg white mix with the chocolate mixture.

Pour the mixture evenly into the prepared ramekins. On a baking sheet, place the ramekins and set them into the oven for about 15 minutes at 350 degrees.

When fluffy and golden, take out of the oven and dust extra sugar over the ramekins, and serve hot.

9. Double Choco Souffle

As I already said, chocolate is one of the most craved delicacies in desserts, so here is another recipe to fulfill your chocolaty cravings. When you love chocolate already so why not have some double fun with it. This double chocolate souffle is all you need to have at the end of a heavy meal.

Ingredients:

Souffle -

- 3 tbsp. unsweetened cocoa
- 1/2 cup plus 2 tbsp. sugar, divided
- 1/8 tsp. salt
- 3 tbsp. all-purpose flour
- 3 ounces bittersweet chocolate, chopped
- 1 tsp. vanilla extract
- 1 1/4 cups fat-free milk
- 6 large egg whites
- 1 large egg yolk
- Cooking spray

Sauce -

- 2 tbsp. unsweetened cocoa
- 1/2 cup fat-free milk
- 1/3 cup sugar
- 1 tbsp. butter
- 1 tbsp. all-purpose flour
- 1/2 ounce bittersweet chocolate, chopped

Serving Size - 6

Cooking Time - 1 hour

Instructions:

Prepare the oven by preheating it to 425 degrees. Take 6 souffle dishes and brush the insides with cooking spray. Keep in the refrigerator until needed.

In a medium saucepan, combine, 3 tbsp. cocoa, 3 tbsp. flour, 1/8 tsp. salt and 1/2 cup sugar. Cook and stir continuously over medium-high flame. Set aside from the heat when the mixture gets thickened. Spoon into a bowl and add the egg yolk and vanilla extract to it.

In a separate bowl, whisk the egg whites till stiff peaks arise. Take about 1/4th of the egg white and fold in with the chocolate mixture and then mix with the leftover mixture. Pour the mixture into the souffle dishes evenly and place in the oven for about 41 minutes. Turn down on a baking tray once the souffle is golden and fluffy.

Make the sauce by first melting the butter in a pan over moderate heat. Add 1 tbsp. flour, 2 tbsp. cocoa, and 1/3 cup sugar to the pan. Whisk in the milk for the mixture to combine. Cook for about a minute while stirring continuously.

Remove from the heat once the mixture gets slightly thickened. Stir in some chocolate and then serve alongside the ready souffles.

10. Make Ahead Berry Souffles

The juicy flavor of berries, when transformed into a creamy delight, gives birth to these amazingly delicious berry souffle. This little muffin-like dessert is going to be on your favorite list, that's for sure. Baffle the minds of your loved ones, with this amazing recipe and show off your baking skills.

Ingredients:

- 3 egg whites
- 1 tsp. melted butter
- 1 tbsp. cornflour
- 3 cups frozen berries, thawed
- 1 tsp. icing sugar
- 1 tsp. vanilla extract
- 1 cup caster sugar, plus extra
- 1/2 cup vanilla ice cream, to serve
- 1 tsp. lemon juice

Serving Size - 4 servings

Cooking Time - 30 minutes

Instructions:

Get the oven ready by preheating it to 200 degrees Celsius. Take 4 ramekins and grease them with butter. Sprinkle the extra caster sugar over them and then set them aside in the refrigerator until needed.

Take a medium-sized saucepan and combine vanilla, 1/2 cup caster sugar, cornstarch, berries, and lemon juice with 1/3 cup water in it. Cook over medium heat for about 2-3 minutes till the berries are soft so that they break down.

In a large bowl, take the egg whites and whisk them with the remaining caster sugar till soft peaks are formed. Fold in 1/4th of the egg white into the berry mixture at first and then fold in the remaining mixture.

Pour this mixture into the prepared ramekins and place inside the preheated oven for about 9-11 minutes till they rise. Turn down in a baking tray and dust with icing sugar.

Serve the souffle with the ice cream alongside.

11. Banana - Lime Souffle

The sweetness of banana, along with a contrasting lime flavor, sounds great, doesn't it? Well, it tastes great too, and if you don't believe me, here's the recipe to make you believe. If you're a fan of banana milkshakes, this banana lime souffle is going to be an excellent choice for you.

Ingredients:

- 3 egg whites
- 2 tsp unsalted butter
- 2 tbsp. shredded coconut, toasted
- 1 banana
- 1/3 cup caster sugar
- 1 tbsp. dark rum
- 1 tbsp. lime juice
- 1 tsp. pure icing sugar, to dust

Serving Size - 4

Cooking Time - 15 minutes

Instructions:

Prepare the oven by preheating it to 190 degrees Celsius. Grease 4 ramekins with butter and dust with caster sugar. Shake off excess sugar from the insides and then place it in the refrigerator until needed.

In a food processor, blend the rum, lime juice, and banana until the puree becomes smooth. Pour into a bowl and keep aside. In a separate bowl, take the egg whites and whisk them till stiff peaks form. Stir in caster sugar while whisking and keep beating till the mixture becomes glossy and stiff.

Take about 1/4th of the egg white mix and fold it into the banana mix. Then slowly fold in the whole banana mix with the egg whites.

Pour the mixture evenly into the prepared ramekins and then sprinkle the shredded coconut over it. Place in a baking tray and then put inside the oven to bake for about 10-13 minutes. Take out of the oven when the souffles are golden and fluffy.

Add the finishing touch by dusting with the icing sugar and more shredded coconut. Serve hot.

12. Passionfruit and Banana Souffle

If you believe in matches made in heaven, nothing could fit the definition better than this fruity combo. A sweet dessert that leaves somewhat a tangy aftertaste, this passionfruit banana souffle recipe is worth trying, I promise.

Ingredients:

- 3 free-range eggs, separated
- 1 tbsp. unsalted butter
- 4-5 passionfruit
- 1/2 cup caster sugar, plus extra for dusting
- 1 tsp. icing sugar, to dust
- 1 ripe banana, mashed

Serving Size - 6

Cooking Size - 30 minutes

Instructions:

Get the oven ready by preheating it to 190 degrees Celsius. Prepare 6 ramekins by greasing them with melted butter and dusting them with caster sugar. Shake off the excess from the insides.

Whisk the yolks from the eggs in a large bowl until the mixture gets smooth and pale. Whisk in passionfruit and mashed banana. In a separate bowl, beat the egg whites until soft peaks form. Stir in the remaining caster sugar and then continue to whisk till the mixture turns glossy. Mix 1/4th of the egg whites into banana mixture with a spoon and then mix the complete mixture.

Divide the mixture evenly into the prepared ramekins and place them on a baking sheet. Put them inside the oven and bake for about 15 minutes until the souffles are golden and puffed.

When baked properly, take the souffle out of the oven and sprinkle icing sugar over them. Serve and enjoy!

13. Choco-Almond Souffle

Wanna steal a taste of heaven? Then what could be better than a nutty, chocolaty sweet treat for yourself? No matter if you are happy, sad, or angry, this choco-almond souffle is the best thing to put a smile on your face. Bake for yourself and find out why I said that.

Ingredients:

- 3 tbsp. unsalted butter
- 6 egg whites
- 7 ounces semi-sweet baking chocolate, chopped
- 2 cups milk
- 1/2 cup granulated sugar
- 1/3 cup all-purpose flour
- 1/8 tsp. salt
- 1/3 cup strong coffee
- 1 tbsp. pure vanilla extract
- 1/2 cup pulverized toasted almonds.
- 1 tsp. powdered sugar
- 1/4 tsp. almond extract
- 4 egg yolks
- 1/2 cup whipped cream, for serving

Serving Size – 4

Cooking Time - 45 minutes

Instructions:

Prepare the oven by preheating it to about 425 degrees Fahrenheit. Also, get 4 souffle dishes (10 ounces) ready by brushing the insides with melted butter.

Mix the coffee and chocolate in a medium-sized heatproof bowl and melt over a pot of simmering water for about 5 minutes. When properly melted, set aside until needed.

Place a medium-sized saucepan over moderate heat and let the butter melt in the pan. Add the flour and stir in milk to form somewhat a smooth cream. Bring to a boil while continuously stirring for 3 minutes. Set aside from heat when the mixture begins to thicken. Add the chocolate mixture and egg yolks to the pan, and whisk to mix everything. Stir in the almond extract, vanilla extract, and almonds, mix well.

Take the egg whites in a separate bowl and whisk well. Stir in salt and granulated sugar and continue to whisk till soft peaks arise. Fold the egg whites into the chocolate mixture using a rubber spatula. Pour the mixture into the prepared souffle dishes and place in the oven to bake at 375 degrees for about 24-29 minutes.

Take out of the oven when the souffle has risen from the dish and the top appears to be cracked. Dust with powdered sugar and top with whipped cream. Serve hot.

14. Twice Baked Goat Cheese Souffle

I know your craving for cheese in everything so here is another cheesy souffle recipe, just for you. Believe it or not, it's even more cheesy than my cheesy lines. So, what are you still thinking? Go and start with your baking right away, your goat cheese souffle is waiting!

Ingredients:

- 2/3 cup finely grated parmesan
- 5 egg whites
- 2 cups milk
- 4 oz goat cheese
- 2 fresh bay leaves
- 6 egg yolks
- 1/2 cup plain flour
- 1 cup butter
- 1 tsp. salt
- 1 tsp. pepper
- 2 pears, cored, thinly sliced
- 1/3 cup verjuice
- 2 tbsp. hazelnut oil
- 1/2 cup hazelnuts
- 3/4 cup extra virgin olive oil
- 1/2 cup rocket leaves

Serving Size – 6

Cooking Time - 45 minutes

Instructions:

Get the oven ready by preheating it to 180 degrees Celsius. Prepare 6 ramekins by brushing them with butter. Take the bay leaves and milk in a medium-sized saucepan and combine over moderate heat. Set aside from heat when the milk begins to simmer.

In a separate saucepan, melt the butter and stir in the flour. Cook for about 3 minutes and then pour the hot milk into the flour. Stir continuously and cook for about 5 minutes till it thickens and boils. Stir in 2 tbsp. of parmesan and goat cheese. Cook for another 3 minutes till the cheese melts.

Season the mixture with pepper and salt after removing it from heat. Take the bay leaves out and keep them aside to cool. Now, to the cheese mixture, add the egg yolks and whisk properly. In another bowl, beat the egg whites till soft peaks form. Mix in the egg whites with the cheese mixture using a spoon to let in air.

Pour the mixture into the prepared ramekins and place in the oven to bake for 21 minutes. When the souffle are golden brown and have risen from the ramekins, take them out and turn them down on a baking tray. Put in the refrigerator while you prepare the salad for serving.

Prepare the pear and rocket salad by first spreading the hazelnuts over a baking tray. Place in the oven for about 10 minutes, take out the lightly toasted hazelnuts, and remove the skins. Chop them coarsely. In a small bowl, combine hazelnut oil with verjuice oil. Sprinkle pepper and salt. Mix the pear, rocket, and hazelnuts in another bowl.

Combine them with half the dressing. Put the souffle back in the oven for 11 minutes at 200 degrees. Remove and serve with the remaining dressing.

15. Mocha Souffle

Winters get so much better with a cup of hot coffee or hot chocolate. But what if we bring both these comforting flavors in a nice and warm dessert! You wished for it and here it is, the perfect recipe to soothe you on those boring winter mornings, a mocha souffle.

Ingredients:

- 3 tbsp. butter, melted
- 3/4 cup strong coffee, hot
- 2 eggs, separated
- 3 tbsp. flour
- 5 tbsp. sugar
- 1/4 tsp. salt
- 3/4 tsp. vanilla
- 2 ounces unsweetened chocolate
- 1 tsp. powdered sugar
- 1/4 cup. heavy cream
- 1/4 tsp. grated nutmeg

Serving Size – 4

Cooking Time - 30 minutes

Instructions:

Prepare the oven by preheating it to 350 degrees. Grease 4 ramekins with melted butter.

Take the egg yolks in a medium-sized bowl and whisk along with sugar for about 5 minutes. Stir in flour, butter, and salt and combine well. In a separate heatproof bowl, take the coffee over the chocolate and whisk it till the chocolate melts. Pour the vanilla and cream into the chocolate mixture and then combine this mixture with the egg yolks. Set aside after whisking for 1 more time.

Take the egg whites in a separate bowl and whisk them till soft peaks arise. Fold the egg whites into the chocolate mixture gently using a spoon to let in the air.

Pour the mixture evenly into the prepared ramekins and then place in the oven for about 32-36 minutes. Take out the oven once the souffle is lightly browned and risen from the ramekins.

Dust with powdered sugar and nutmeg. Serve while it's hot.

16. Gruyere Cheese Souffle

Soft in the center, fluffy on the outside, and with the aroma of Gruyere cheese filling your kitchen, can you imagine how yummy it will be. Stop imagining, for I have the recipe right here. Now get up and rush for the ingredients before your watering mouth brings a flood.

Ingredients:

- 5 large eggs, separated
- 3 1/2 tbsp. all-purpose flour
- 3 tbsp. unsalted butter
- 1/2 tsp. kosher salt
- 1 cup cold milk
- 3 ounces Gruyere cheese, 1 cup shredded
- 2 tbsp. freshly grated Parmigiano-Reggiano cheese
- 1/2 tsp. freshly ground pepper
- 2 slices of yellow American cheese, each cut into 6 strips
- 2 tbsp. chopped chives

Serving Size - 4

Cooking Time - 1 hour

Instructions:

Prepare the oven by preheating it to 4000 degrees. Also, get ready for 4 souffle plates or ramekins and grease each of them with the melted butter and sprinkle the Parmigiano on the insides. Shake off the excess Parmigiano and set aside till needed.

Melt about 3 tbsp. butter in a saucepan over medium flame. Add the flour to the pan and whisk well and cook for about a minute. Stir in the milk and cook until it boils and gets thickened. Set aside from the flames and then add 4 egg yolks to the pan. Season with pepper and salt and whisk well.

Take the egg whites in a separate bowl and beat them well till stiff peaks arise. Fold in 1/3 of the egg whites into the egg yolk mixture and then gently fold in the complete egg white mixture. Add the chives and Gruyere, and fold them into the mixture.

Pour the mixture into the prepared ramekins and top with the American cheese in a zigzag pattern. Place the ramekins inside the oven and bake for about 24 minutes. Take them out when the souffles are golden and puffed.

Serve immediately.

17. Raspberry Souffle

As beautiful as it looks, this exquisite raspberry souffle tastes just as good. The juicy raspberries bring a perfect contrast to the classic dish and you can't resist taking another bite. So, what are you waiting for? Get going with your baking.

Ingredients:

- 4 large egg yolks
- 12 ounces frozen raspberry, thawed
- 1 1/2 tbsp. cornstarch
- 4 egg whites
- 1 tbsp. lemon juice
- 3 1/2 ounces granulated sugar
- 1 tsp. powdered sugar
- 4-5 fresh raspberries for garnishing
- 1 tbsp. melted butter
- 1 tsp. Kosher salt
- 1 tbsp. cream of tartar

Serving Size - 4

Cooking Time - 35 minutes

Instructions:

Get the oven ready by preheating it to 400 degrees Fahrenheit. Take 4 ramekins, brush them with butter, and dust with granulated sugar on the insides. Shake off the excess sugar from the inside and set them aside on a baking sheet.

Put the thawed raspberries in a food processor to prepare the puree. Sieve the seeds from the puree and set aside the smooth puree in a bowl. In another bowl, take the egg yolks and whisk well while adding cornstarch and sugar. Continue whisking till the mixture is pale and thick. Stir in lemon juice and raspberry puree. Keep aside for a while.

In a separate bowl, take the cream of tartar with the egg whites and add some salt to it. Whisk well, adding some granulated sugar in between. Continue to whisk till firm peaks form.

Fold in 1/3 of the egg whites into the egg yolk mixture and then fold the complete egg white mixture in it. Gently pour the mixture into the prepared ramekins. Place the ramekins in the preheated oven for about 15-21 minutes and then take them out when lightly browned at the souffle tops.

Add the finishing touch by garnishing with fresh raspberries and dusting with powdered sugar. Serve hot.

18. Eggless Kiwi Souffle

Now, don't get sad if you're a vegan. Like I said in the beginning we have varieties for each and everyone, so here's one for you too. An eggless kiwi souffle is the perfect choice for a healthy vegan diet. Not only that, this chilled dessert is a great choice for everyone the summers are getting tough to deal with.

Ingredients:

- 1/2 cup milk
- 1 tbsp. grated chocolate
- 3/4 cup Kiwi crush or fresh kiwis (finely chopped)
- 2 slices of extra kiwi
- 2 tbsp. chopped almonds
- 1 cup vanilla ice-cream
- 1/4 cup milkmaid
- 2 sprigs of mint

Serving Size - 2

Cooking Time - 15 minutes

Instructions:

In a large bowl, take the crushed kiwis, chopped almonds, grated chocolate, milk, vanilla ice cream, and milkmaid. Whisk everything together until smooth.

Take 2 ice cream bowls and pour the mixture into them. Place the kiwi pieces on top and decorate with the mint sprigs. Use foil paper to cover the cups.

Place the cups in the freezer and let them freeze for about 3-4 hours.

Take them out of the freezer and serve your chilled souffle immediately.

19. Chicken and Cheddar Souffle

A spicy yet light appetizer, this chicken cheddar souffle is the best option you can choose. Great to taste yet keeps space in your stomach for the main course, you're gonna love these little delights. Try baking once and this will become a constant for every family dinner.

Ingredients:

- 2 packed cups of baby spinach leaves
- 1/4 cup all-purpose flour
- 1/2 tsp. ground nutmeg
- 1 1/2 cups shredded mild cheddar
- 4 tbsp. unsalted butter
- 1/2 cup grated parmesan
- 1 tsp. kosher salt
- 1 tsp. freshly ground pepper
- 1 1/2 cups whole milk
- 6 egg yolks, lightly beaten
- 2 cups rotisserie chicken, cut into 1/2 inch cubes
- 6 egg whites
- 2 country-style white bread, cut into 1/2 inch cubes

Serving Size - 4

Cooking Time - 1 hour 10 minutes

Instructions:

Prepare 4 ramekins with a 10-ounce capacity by brushing butter on the insides. Also, keep the oven preheated to 400 degrees Fahrenheit. Keep the ramekins aside till needed.

Melt about 1 tbsp. butter over moderate heat in a medium-sized saucepan. Stir in the flour and cook for about 3 minutes. Add the milk and continue to stir till the mixture turns creamy and smooth. Let it simmer for about 7-9 minutes. Add the salt, pepper, and nutmeg, and stir well.

Set aside from heat and then add the chicken, cheeses, egg yolks, spinach, cheddar, and bread cubes and mix well. Make sure all the ingredients get combined.

Take the egg whites in a separate bowl and beat for about 3 minutes until soft peaks form. Fold in a quarter of the whites into the base mixture and then stir in the remaining egg whites too. Pour the mixture into the prepared ramekins and then place in the preheated oven. Bake for about an hour till the souffle rises from the ramekins, all fluffy and lightly browned.

Remove from oven once baked properly and then serve hot. Enjoy!

20. Grand Marnier Souffle

Confused about how to make your romantic date night more special. I've got you! Bake them these delicious Grand Marnier souffle and watch them fall in love with you all over again. Even I can't explain why this lovely dessert is the showstopper for any occasion.

Ingredients:

- 2 egg yolks
- 5 tsp. all-purpose flour
- 1 tbsp. plus 5 tsp. melted butter
- 1/4 cup cold milk
- 1 tbsp. brandy-based orange liqueur
- 1 tbsp. plus 1/4 cup white sugar
- 2 egg whites
- 1/8 tsp. vanilla extract
- 1 tsp. freshly grated orange zest

Serving Size - 2

Cooking Time - 50 minutes

Instructions:

Prepare 2 ramekins with 8-ounce capacity by brushing the insides with melted butter. Get the oven preheated to 400 degrees Fahrenheit. Set the ramekins aside on a baking tray.

In a medium-sized saucepan, melt about 1 tbsp. and 2 tsp. butter over moderate heat. Add the flour and sugar into the saucepan and cook for about 3 minutes till the butter turns light brown. Stir in milk and cook for about 5 more minutes till the mixture turns thick and smooth.

Set the pan aside from the heat and then pour it into a bowl. Add the orange liqueur and orange zest to the bowl and stir till they get combined. Stir in the vanilla extract and egg yolks too. Make sure the mixture is smooth enough.

In a separate bowl, take the egg whites and whisk well. Stir in half of the 1/4 cup sugar into the bowl and continue to whisk till soft peaks arise. Fold a quarter of this mixture into the previous bowl and then fold the remaining egg whites into the bowl using a spoon. Pour this mixture evenly into the prepared ramekins and place it on the baking tray.

Bake for about 15 minutes till the souffle rise from the ramekins and the tops become golden brown. Remove from the oven and serve immediately.

21. Lemon Souffle

Sounds simple but trust me, the simple ones turn out to be the extraordinary ones. This lemon souffle will leave such a taste that you are going to fall in love with this dessert. It may not be that sweet but it's just sweet enough to melt in your mouth.

Ingredients:

- 1 cup milk
- 3 tbsp. all-purpose flour
- 4 eggs, separated, plus 1 egg white
- 2 tbsp. unsalted butter
- 2 tbsp. lemon zest
- 1/2 cup fresh lemon juice
- 1 tsp. confectioner's sugar
- 1/2 cup sugar, plus more for dusting

Serving Size - 4

Cooking Time - 50 minutes

Instructions:

Get the oven preheated to 375 degrees Fahrenheit. Also, prepare 4 ramekins by brushing the insides with butter and dusting with sugar. Keep them aside on a baking tray until needed.

Place a saucepan over medium heat and add the flour, 1/4 cup sugar, egg yolks, and zest. Stir in the milk and cook for about 10 minutes till the mixture turns creamy and thick. Remove from the heat and transfer to a bowl. Add the lemon juice and butter, and stir well.

Take the egg whites in a separate bowl and then whisk till soft peaks form. Stir in the remaining sugar and continue whisking till the peaks stiffen. Fold in about a quarter of the egg whites into the lemon mixture and then gently stir in the remaining egg whites too.

Divide this mixture evenly among the previously prepared ramekins and place inside the oven for about 20 minutes. Remove from the oven once the souffle is golden brown and puffed.

Serve immediately after dusting with the confectioner's sugar.

22. Classic Spinach Souffle

Who said healthy can't be yummy! Here's one proof I have to prove that wrong. This spinach souffle is going to fit perfectly into your diet and you're gonna love it too. Try this classic and see for yourself.

Ingredients:

- 2 tbsp. all-purpose flour
- 3 tbsp. freshly grated parmesan
- 1 cup whole milk
- 1 pound stemmed and chopped spinach
- 1/8 tsp. nutmeg
- 5 1/2 tbsp. unsalted butter
- 3 large eggs
- 1/2 tsp. Kosher salt
- 1/8 tsp. freshly ground pepper

Serving Size - 4

Cooking Time - 65 minutes

Instructions:

Get the oven preheated to 375 degrees Fahrenheit. Take 4 souffle dishes and prepare them by brushing the insides with butter. Dust the surface with some parmesan cheese too. Shake off the excess and keep them aside on a baking tray till needed.

Add the chopped spinach to a medium saucepan heated to moderate flames. Let the liquid evaporate from the spinach and cook till the leaves wilt. Make sure the spinach doesn't burn. Remove from heat once cooked. Strain the excess juices if something remains.

Place another medium-sized saucepan over moderate heat and let the remaining butter melt in the pan. Add salt and flour, and cook for half a minute while stirring continuously. Pour the milk and cook for another 5 minutes while stirring continuously till the mixture becomes thick enough. Stir in the spinach and season with salt and pepper. Add nutmeg and continue cooking for about 2 minutes.

Take the egg yolks in a large bowl and stir in 1/2 cup of spinach mixture into the bowl from the pan. Transfer this egg mixture to the pan and cook while stirring it. Remove from heat when completely incorporated. Make sure not to overheat or else the eggs may separate.

In a separate bowl, take the egg whites and beat until firm peaks rise. Fold in 1/4 of this mixture into the pan and then gently fold in the remaining egg whites with the spinach mixture too. Pour this mixture into the prepared souffle dishes and then place inside the oven.

Bake for about 25-31 minutes and remove from the oven once the souffle is golden brown and puffed. Serve hot and enjoy your treat!

23. Vanilla Souffle with Ice-Cream

The dessert menu seems so incomplete without ice cream, at least for me it does. And that's why this recipe is my personal favorite. A classic French dessert with an icy twist. Try this and this vanilla souffle will become your favorite too.

Ingredients:

- 1/2 vanilla bean, split lengthwise and scraped
- 2 tbsp. unsalted butter
- 3/4 cup plus 2 tbsp. all-purpose flour
- 2 cups whole milk
- 1/4 tsp. salt
- 1 large egg white
- 1/3 cup plus 1/4 cup granulated sugar, plus more for dishes
- 4 large eggs, separated
- 1 tsp. Confectioner's sugar
- 1 tsp. pure vanilla extract
- 1/4 tsp. cream of tartar
- 4 scoop Vanilla-bean ice cream

Serving Size - 4

Cooking Time - 45 minutes

Instructions:

Prepare 4 souffle dishes by brushing with butter on the insides, also dusting with sugar. Mix the vanilla bean and milk in a medium saucepan over high heat. Let the milk boil and then set aside from the heat. Discard the bean from the milk and then set it aside for some other use, while covering and storing the milk.

Mix the salt, 1/3 cup granulated sugar, and flour in a bowl. Pour the reserved milk and whisk well to make the mixture a paste. Add the pasta to a saucepan and cook with the milk over moderate heat for about 6-7 minutes while whisking continuously. Set aside from heat when the mixture becomes perfectly smooth.

Add the vanilla extract with the egg yolks to the saucepan and whisk well until combined properly. Take the egg whites to another bowl and beat along with the cream of tartar till the mixture gets foamy. Stir in 1/4 cup sugar to the bowl and continue whisking till soft peaks form.

Fold in a quarter of the egg white into the egg yolk mixture at first and then gently fold in the remaining mixture. Pour evenly into the prepared dishes and then place the dishes on a baking tray. Transfer the tray to an oven preheated to 375 degrees and let the souffle bake for about 15-21 minutes. Take out when scuffles appear to be, puffed and golden brown.

Add the finishing touch by dusting Confectioner's sugar. Serve alongside the vanilla-bean ice cream.

24. Potato Souffle

Here's another savory recipe amidst all the sweetness that can be your favorite even if you're more of a sweet tooth. The only veggie that goes well with everything, potatoes never fail to impress. This classic yet yummy dish won't disappoint you, I assure you.

Ingredients:

- 2 large eggs, separated
- 2 tbsp. unsalted butter
- 3 tbsp. heavy cream
- 1 cup leftover mashed potatoes
- 3 tbsp. grated parmesan cheese
- 3 tbsp. fine dried bread crumbs
- 1/2 tsp. minced garlic
- 1 tsp. freshly grated nutmeg
- Salt and freshly ground pepper, 1 tsp. each

Serving Size - 4

Cooking Time - 30 minutes

Instructions:

Firstly, the oven should be preheated to 375 degrees. Then prepare 4 ramekins by brushing the insides with butter. Dust with bread crumbs and keep aside till needed.

Take the egg yolks, potatoes, garlic, cream, and parmesan cheese together in a bowl and whisk till the mixture is well combined and creamy. Keep the mixture aside after seasoning with pepper and salt.

In a separate bowl, take the egg whites with some salt and whisk till soft peaks form. Fold a quarter of this mixture into the potato base and then fold the complete egg white mixture into the base.

Divide this mixture evenly into the prepared ramekins and then place in the preheated oven. Bake for about 41 minutes till the souffle become puffy and golden in color.

Take out when properly baked, and add the finishing touch with the nutmeg on top of the souffle. Serve immediately.

25. Carrot Souffle

No, you aren't a rabbit if you love carrots. If you love carrots, here's one recipe you have to try for yourself. A sweet and simple dessert, this carrot souffle is a lovely choice for a lovely evening.

Ingredients:

- 1 cup whole milk
- 1/3 cup minced onion
- 2 lbs. carrots, peeled and sliced
- 3/4 cup grated cheddar cheese
- 1/8 tsp. cayenne
- 1 cup Saltine cracker crumbs
- 1 tsp. Kosher salt
- 3 large eggs
- 1 tsp. salt for salting water
- 1 tbsp. unsalted butter
- 1/4 tsp. black pepper

Serving Size - 8

Cooking Time - 80 minutes

Instructions:

Get the oven ready by preheating it to 350 degrees. Prepare a 2-quart baking dish by brushing it with butter. Keep aside until needed.

In a saucepan, take the carrots and pour almost an inch of water to cover them. Stir in salt and cook the carrots for about 9 minutes in the boiling water at medium heat. Remove from heat once the carrots seem tender. Strain the water and put the carrots in a blender. Prepare a carrot puree and transfer it to a large bowl.

Add the grated cheese, Saltine crumbs, milk, butter, onion, black pepper, cayenne, and kosher salt to the puree and whisk well. Make sure the mixture is completely smooth with no lumps left in it.

Take the eggs to another bowl and then whisk until they turn frothy. Further, add the eggs to the puree base and whisk again. Pour this mixture into the baking dish you prepared earlier. Place in the preheated oven and let the souffle bake for about 41-44 minutes at 350 degrees Fahrenheit.

Remove from the oven once the souffle becomes lightly golden and puffed. Serve immediately and enjoy your carrot souffle!

26. Apple Souffle

How can we forget apples when we're talking about all kinds of fruity desserts here. So here is a recipe for a nice and yummy apple souffle too. Experiment with your baking skills and see how good this version of the dish turns out to be.

Ingredients:

- 1 tbsp. potato starch
- 2 tbsp. sugar
- 6 eggs, separated
- 1 tsp. Kosher salt
- 1 tsp. cinnamon
- 2 tbsp. canola oil
- 6 apples, cored, peeled

Serving Size - 4

Cooking Time - 1 hour

Instructions:

Get the oven ready by preheating it to 400 degrees Fahrenheit. Brush 4 ramekins with the canola oil and set aside until needed.

In a large bowl, take the egg yolks and whisk well until smooth. Stir in the salt, sugar, potato starch, cinnamon, and apple slices, and continue whisking till everything is well combined.

Take the egg whites in a separate bowl and beat well till soft peaks form. Fold 1/4 of this egg white mixture into the apple mixture and then gently fold in the remaining egg whites too.

Divide the mixture evenly among the prepared ramekins and place in the preheated oven for about 36 minutes.

Take out once the souffle is well baked and puffed. Serve hot and enjoy!

27. Yam Souffle

If you're someone who loves trying unique stuff, then you should try this yam souffle. It may sound weird here but once you try it, you can't even imagine how surprised you are going to be.

Ingredients:

- 40 ounces large yams
- 1 tsp. ground cinnamon
- 1 tbsp. butter
- 1/2 cup chopped pecans
- 12-ounce marshmallow topping
- 1 cup light brown sugar
- 1 tsp. ground nutmeg

Serving Size - 8

Cooking Time - 40 minutes

Instructions:

Get the oven preheated to 325 degrees Fahrenheit. Brush a metal pie pan with butter and keep aside until needed.

In a medium saucepan, add the butter and let it melt over moderate flames. Stir in pecans and brown sugar. Cook for about 4 minutes while stirring continuously and then set aside from the heat.

Drain the yams and transfer them to a large bowl. Mash the yams in that bowl leaving only little chunks behind. Add the sugar mixture to the yams and combine everything well. Stir in nutmeg and cinnamon, and mix well.

Pour this mixture into the prepared pie pan and then add the marshmallow toppings on top. Place in the preheated oven and bake for about 16 minutes. Take the pan out of the oven and increase the temperature to 400 from 325. Place it inside again for 11 more minutes and remove once the top is brown enough.

Serve immediately!

28. Corn Souffle

As simple as a pie! Wouldn't it be great if you could apply that sentence to souffles too? Well, with this corn souffle recipe, you can surely say so because it is even simpler than you think.

Ingredients:

- 1 cup sour cream
- 15 Oz creamed corn with liquid
- 1/2 cup melted butter
- 15 Oz corn kernels
- 8-ounce Jiffy corn muffin mix, unprepared

Serving Size - 2

Cooking Time - 1 hour

Instructions:

Get the oven ready by preheating it to 350 degrees. Prepare 2 a square 9-inch baking tray by brushing butter on the insides.

Take the sour cream, corn kernels, corn muffin mix, creamed corn, and remaining butter in a large bowl and mix well until smooth.

Pour the mixture into the prepared tray and then place the tray in the oven for about 45-51 minutes. Bake till the souffles are lightly browned and nice.

Remove from the oven once properly baked and then serve immediately.

29. Strawberry Ricotta Souffle

This strawberry ricotta souffle will tickle your taste buds in such a way that it'll be hard to keep yourself away from them. Taste once and fall in love for the rest of your life.

Ingredients:

- 4 eggs divided
- 2 tbsp. flour
- 15 Oz. part-skim ricotta cheese
- 3 tbsp. unseasoned dry bread crumbs
- 1/4 cup toasted almonds, chopped
- 1 tsp. powdered sugar for garnishing
- 1/2 cup granulated sugar
- 1 tbsp. softened butter

Serving Size - 8

Cooking Time - 1 hour

Instructions:

Prepare an 8-inch souffle dish by brushing the insides with butter and then dusting granulated sugar over it. Shake off excess sugar from the inside and keep it aside until needed. Get the oven preheated to 375 degrees Fahrenheit.

Take the 1/3 cup sugar, ricotta cheese, egg yolks, flour, and breadcrumbs in a medium-sized bowl. Mix thoroughly until all the ingredients get combined. Set aside for a while.

Blend the egg whites in a separate bowl till soft peaks form. With the help of a spoon, fold this egg white mixture into the cheese mixture.

Transfer the mixture to the prepared souffle dish and place it in the preheated oven for about 41-46 minutes. Remove from the oven once the souffle is golden brown and well baked.

Garnish with powdered sugar and almonds. Serve immediately.

30. Blintz Souffle

With this recipe, we have come to the end of this cookbook but as they say, save the best for the last, so here it is. Bake this blintz souffle for your loved ones and watch the big smile it brings to their face.

Ingredients:

- 3 eggs
- 2 tbsp. butter
- 13 Oz frozen blintzes
- 2 tbsp. sugar
- 1/2 cup sour cream
- 1 tsp. vanilla
- 2 tbsp. orange juice

Serving Size - 6

Cooking Time - 1 hour

Instructions:

Get the oven preheated to 375 degrees Fahrenheit. Prepare a baking pan by brushing the insides with the melted butter. Pour the blintzes into the pan and spread at the bottom.

In a food processor, take the other ingredients and then blend till you get a smooth puree. Add this puree to the pan right above the blintzes.

Place the pan in the preheated oven and bake for about 16 minutes. Reduce the temperature to 350 degrees from 375 and then bake for another 36-46 minutes.

Remove from the oven once it becomes brown and puffy. Serve immediately.

Conclusion:

As I end this cookbook, I hope that all the recipes here will turn out to be a great help for you. Souffles may be a bit tricky to bake at times but always remember that it all depends on the cooking time. Have patience and good observation, your souffle is going to be just as perfect as you've thought of.

So, what are you waiting for? Go grab your utensils and ingredients, choose the one recipe you love, and start baking. Of course, you'll love more than one, that's for sure but take time to learn as this dish can be difficult to perfect. But I know, with a pinch of love added to the ingredients, you'll surely work your magic on it. Happy Baking!

Epilogues

There are days I feel like quitting, but then I remember readers like you, and my heart swells with pride at the love you show me by buying each and every book I put out there.

I am delighted, to say the least, to know that people like you take their time to download, read and cook with my books!

Thank you so much for accepting me and all that I have shared with the world.

While I am basking in the euphoria of your love and commitment to my books, I would beseech you to kindly drop your reviews and feedback. I would love to read from you!

Head to Amazon.com to drop your reviews!!!

Thank you

Charlotte Long

About the Author

For the past 10 years, Charlotte has been collating and exploring different dishes from different cultures of the world. Birthed and raised in Ohio, Charlotte grew up to know that cooking is a magical activity that requires a certain degree of commitment and love to be carried out.

She learnt this from her grandmother who was one of the best local chefs in Ohio then. Charlotte's grandmother would always create and invent new recipes and also refurbish old ones. The result of it is her passion for cooking cum a large book of special recipes that Charlotte inherited.

Using her grandmother's recipe book as her foundational training guide, Charlotte wore her grandmother's chef shoes to become one of the best chefs in Ohio and its environment.

Charlotte has written different recipe books, and she is currently touring the Caribbean and looking for new recipes to unravel.

♡♡♡♡♡♡♡♡♡♡♡♡♡♡♡

Printed in Great Britain
by Amazon

d77fe524-f1b7-471c-a1a4-ebd524a04645R01